Growing Up Indian

Growing Up Indian

Evelyn Wolfson

Illustrated by William Sauts Bock

Walker and Company
New York

First published in the United States of America
in 1986 by the Walker Publishing Company, Inc.

Published simultaneously in Canada by John Wiley & Sons
Canada, Limited, Rexdale, Ontario.

Library of Congress Cataloging-in-Publication Data

Wolfson, Evelyn.
  Growing up Indian.

  Summary: Uses question and answer format to describe
life for Indian children long ago, as they learned to
preserve their culture and prepared for adulthood.
  1. Indians of North America—Children—Juvenile
literature. 2. Indians of North America—Youth—
Juvenile literature. [1. Indians of North America—
Social life and customs. 2. Questions and answers]
I. Bock, William Sauts, 1939–   ill. II. Title.
E98.C5W68   1986   306′.08997073   86-9053
ISBN 0-8027-6643-9
ISBN 0-8027-6644-7 (lib. bdg.)

Printed in the United States of America

10 9 8 7 6 5 4 3 2 1

Many thanks to my friend, Sandy Hoyt, for her perpetual assistance and encouragement

Contents

Introduction

DID YOU EVER WISH you could run free with the Indians of long ago? Indian children never had to take naps. They could eat whenever they got hungry. And they were seldom spanked. Indian children didn't have to go to school. Yet they grew up to be responsible, contributing members of their communities.

What Indian children learned was very important, because it prepared them to take care of themselves and their families. Their learning did not have to take place in school. Everything they needed to know, they could observe being done by adults around them. Children enjoyed doing the same things the grown-ups did.

Children moved freely around their villages, exploring and experimenting on their own. They were given guidance and help only when needed. Play was an important part of their daily activities and was not separate from learning.

Children developed confidence and a sense of worth by making small versions of the tools and utensils used by adults for hunting, fishing, and gathering food. Adults made dolls and little canoes for children to play with. And they taught them how to have fun playing games that were exciting and that helped to sharpen their physical and mental skills.

This book tells how Indian children were cared for as babies, how they learned to preserve their culture by watching and doing and by listening to stories told by their elders. It describes the games they played and the toys they used. It explains how they lived, what they wore, and how they prepared for adulthood.

Indian people today still enjoy many aspects of their old culture, even though their lives have changed. Some Indian people now prefer to be called Native Americans.

A YOUNG BOY LEARNING TO SPEAR FISH.

Growing Up Indian

KIOWA CRADLEBOARD

FROM CRADLEBOARD to MOCCASIN

What is a cradleboard?

Papooses stayed with their mothers all the time. An Indian baby was usually carried in a cradleboard on its mother's back, strapped securely in place like a cocoon on a limb. Most cradleboards were made out of a flat piece of wood that had holes up the side for lacing. There was a footrest at the bottom and a hoop on top of each cradleboard to protect the baby's head. Cradleboards could be moved easily from place to place and even propped against a tree or a post near camp. When there was work to be done in the garden, the mother hung the cradleboard from the limb of a tree, away from curious animals. High off the ground, babies watched broad green treetips brush the blue of the sky, and they listened to their mothers sing as they worked.

1

DELAWARE BABY WITH TOY BIRD SKULL

Newborn babies were sometimes carried around on a simple undecorated wooden board. When they were six months old, they were given a sturdy wooden cradleboard made by their fathers, or a tightly woven cradleboard made by their mothers. Layers of finely shredded bark, covered with thick, fluffy animal furs, served as cradleboard mattresses.

**PAIUTE WOVEN CRADLEBOARD
WITH BUCKSKIN COVER**

Babies did not wear clothes. Instead, they were wrapped in warm furs, then laced securely in place with fancy lacing made from narrow strips of animal skin. Skin lacing was often decorated with brightly colored beads. Most of the time, the cradleboards were laced all the way up past the babies' shoulders, so only their heads remained uncovered. At other times, their arms were left free, so they could play with the tiny handmade toys tied to the cradleboard hoop. Babies loved to touch the little bird skulls, turtle-shell rattles, and elk-horn spoons made by their fathers, and the tiny clay animals made by their mothers, who hoped the animals they created would protect their babies.

Fresh animal bones were tied to babies' wrists when they were teething. During maple-sugaring season in the Northeast, babies chewed on small leather pouches filled with maple sugar. The pouches were sewn together very loosely, so the sugar seeped out easily.

Did babies wear diapers?

Indian babies did not have cloth diapers, but they were kept dry with diaper-like material gathered from the out-of-doors. Soft bundles of damp, spongy moss were collected in the woods, then spread in the sun to dry. In autumn, the furry brown seed-heads from the cattail plant were collected from marshes. When the seed-heads dried and were pulled apart, thousands of fluffy white "parachutes" were released. The "parachutes," designed to carry the tiny brown seeds on a windward journey, are as soft and absorbent as modern-day cotton. Both moss and cattail seed-heads were stored in baskets for use all year.

Several times a day, babies had their diapers changed when mothers relined the cradleboard with dry moss or cattail down. Since babies did not move

ARAPAHO BLANKET CARRIER

around very much, this method of diapering served just as well as modern wraparound diapers. Diapering time gave babies a chance to kick their legs and get some exercise. At night, babies were taken off the cradleboards and put to sleep with their parents on a flat mat or fur robe.

Indian parents believed cradleboards gave children straight, sturdy legs that made them fast runners.

When babies began to crawl, they were no longer laced onto their cradleboards each day, but were dressed in tiny animal skin moccasins. Chippewa parents, living around Lakes Huron and Superior, cut small holes in the moccasins to show the spirits their child needed new shoes, "to hurry it to walk." Holes also were to show the spirits that the moccasins were in such bad condition that a baby could not be expected to take a long journey in them.

Around the campsite, babies were often carried in blanket hammocks tied around their mothers' waists. Very young babies were carried near their mothers' chests, while older children were supported on their mothers' backs.

4

How were they named?

Babies born today have names given to them right away. Modern Americans often choose their favorite names for their babies or select names that remind them of people they like or of a favorite relative. Some people name their first son after his father, adding "Junior" to the name. But Indian babies were seldom given names when they were born. In fact, it wasn't considered important for Indians to have names—and certainly not names that would stay with them for life. When the settlers came to America, many Indians liked the odd-sounding English names and changed their own. Alexander, King Philip, and Chief Joseph are only a few famous Indians who changed their names. The Indian custom of name-changing caused much confusion for the settlers, but was perfectly natural for the Indians.

Indian babies were often called "Little Girl," "Little Boy," or just plain "Baby" for the first five years. A name meant a number of different things and was changed all the time. A boy might be called "Boy" for five or six years, then be called "Fleeing Feet of the Prairie" after he had shot his first small animal. A girl who learned to weave when she was very young might be called "Nimble Fingers" for a period of time.

Among tribes of the Maidu, who lived in northeastern California, children were not named until they were three years old. Then they were given a name that described their actions or mannerisms. A very active little girl might be called "Climbing Girl" or, if she made noise when she slept, "Snoring Bird." Sometimes a child's name described a particular place the family had visited. A family who returned to a favorite fishing spot each spring might call their son "Boy of the Salmon Stream."

5

**A NAVAJO WOMAN WHISPERS A NAME TO
THE MEDICINE MAN.**

Some names described deeds done by parents or
grandparents. A child might be called "Warrior of the
Snow," because his father helped defeat another tribe
in winter. If a woman was an exceptionally good pot-
ter, her daughter might be called "Clay From the Fingers of the Wind." At other times, names described
animals or objects important to the tribe. Boys could
be named after fierce animals such as buffaloes or
bears, but girls could not. They were given the names
of shy, gentle animals such as minks and beavers.

Some tribes considered a name to be private, and
only the child's mother or father could use the name.
Everyone else called the child by a term of relationship like "Sister," "Brother," or "Cousin." Or they
made up a nickname.

Among tribes of the Iroquois, who lived east of Lake
Ontario, individual family groups owned certain names
which no one else could use. Thus, when a person
wanted a name, he had to go to the person in charge
of names and get one that was not in use.

Clans of the Navajo living in Arizona, New Mexico, and Utah, used nicknames, because real names related to war and were considered sacred. Names were not spoken except by medicine men during important ceremonies. When a medicine man wanted to use a name, he had to go to the woman of the house, who took him aside and whispered the name in his ear. It was important that she keep the name a secret until it was needed.

Chippewa babies were named at a special gathering given for friends and relatives. Food and tobacco were offered to the spirits, and a man was chosen to name the baby. The namer usually gave the baby his own name. This insured parents that their child would grow up to be strong, brave, and healthy just like the namer. From then on, the two enjoyed a very special relationship and even called each other "Namesake."

In Wisconsin, a Kickapoo baby was named during the ceremonial season following its birth. This was appropriate because it was a time of feasting and prayer for the tribe.

Tribes of the Northwest named babies at potlatches. A potlatch was a gift-giving celebration hosted by a family, kin group, or other local group. Instead of bringing gifts, the guests were given gifts. This gave the host an opportunity to show off his wealth. Guests, however, were expected to host potlatches of their own. Potlatches helped to redistribute the wealth of a clan or group.

Sometimes when a baby was fretful for no reason, its mother believed it was because the child did not like its name. So she gave it a new name.

YOUNG CHILDREN DO THEIR CHORES—CARRYING
WATER, PICKING BERRIES, AND BRINGING HOME
FIREWOOD.

TODDLERS
at HOME

Who took care of them?

When a baby started to walk, it was free to roam the campsite on its own. All women in the tribe watched toddlers and helped with their care. Older children played with them, grandparents made them toys, and everyone guided them in their explorations. If they tried to leave the campsite or were headed for trouble, an older child or an adult redirected them.

Boys and girls stayed with the women of the tribe until they were five or six years old. They helped gather wild foods, bring in firewood, carry small containers of drinking water, or deliver messages. They learned to obey their elders and to treat them with great respect. They knew at a very young age that misbehavior brought ridicule and rejection. Good behavior brought praise, love, and respect.

**GHOSTLEG IS PUSHED THROUGH THE WIGWAM DOOR
TO FRIGHTEN A CRYING CHILD.**

How were they disciplined?

By the time a child got out of its cradleboard, it had already been disciplined. It knew that crying was a very serious offense. Crying could scare away game and cause a tribe to starve, or it could alert the enemy and bring on a surprise attack. When a baby was only a few days old, its mother gently held its nose at the first signs of crying. The baby learned quickly when not to cry. If a baby cried without reason, it was taken far away where it could not be heard. The cradleboard was set against a tree and left there until the baby was quiet. The threat of being removed from camp was enough to stop most babies from crying without reason.

In fact, threats were one of the most effective forms of discipline for Indian children. Spanking was almost unheard of. Being captured by creatures of the night, like the owl and coyote—animals seldom seen but often heard—was a commonly used threat. The coyote was particularly threatening, because it was a popular figure who could be either a hero or a trickster.

Chippewa children were threatened with ghostleg—a moccasin stuffed with grass and attached to the end of a long pole. When a child misbehaved, ghostleg appeared through the wigwam door. The mere threat of calling for ghostleg made them behave!

Zuni children were threatened with a wild-haired woman called Su'ukyi, who crept through villages at night carrying a packbasket. She could carry away a naughty child on her back, no matter how large it was.

A child was punished—and even publicly humiliated—for using bad judgment, especially if it meant endangering a human life. The punishment for such behavior was to be dunked in an icy stream or to have cold water thrown in the face. This was terribly embarrassing, because everyone in the tribe came to watch.

Children living in the Northeast were disciplined by being made to stand outside the family wigwam with their faces painted black. This was terribly embarrassing since other children made fun of their condition.

Children living in the Southeast were reminded by their parents each day how to behave properly. This prevented them from saying they forgot.

How did they dress?

Most young children did not wear clothing until they were five or six years old, unless it was cold. In the hot desert regions of the Southwest, however, boys didn't bother to wear any clothes at all until they were nine or ten years old. On the other hand, girls wore small breechcloths when they were six years old. A breechcloth is a strip of buckskin, or a piece of cloth, about a foot wide and six feet long. It is passed between the legs and tucked into a waistband in front and in back. Sometimes a simple apron was worn instead. As girls grew up, they wore decorated shirts and long skirts or soft buckskin jumpers.

In the Pacific Northwest, children wore clothing woven out of cedar bark or basswood bark fibers.

In northern regions where it is cold in winter, children wore the same type of clothing as their parents. Men wore long-sleeved shirts, loose-fitting leggings, and heavy moosehide moccasins. Sometimes a piece of fur and another pair of moccasins were put on over the first pair. Women wore skin dresses tied at the waist and long, fitted leggings. Sometimes the leggings were fastened to their moccasins. When it was very cold, everyone wore thick fur robes or blankets over their heads and shoulders.

AN APACHE GIRL WEARS A DECORATED BUCKSKIN OUTFIT.

12

**A NORTHWEST COAST YOUTH WEARS A WOVEN
CEDAR BARK HAT.**

A NORTHERN BOY WEARS A HOODED BLANKET-COAT.

What did they eat?

Children ate whenever they were hungry. Mothers kept a pot of stew on the fire all the time, and served it to the children in small bowls. When they were in a hurry, children were allowed to eat right from the ladle like the adults did.

On the plains and in the woodlands of the North, children ate plenty of deer, elk, moose, and buffalo meat. Most tribes also ate the meat of small animals like rabbits, raccoons, and birds. In the Northwest,

children ate lots of smoked salmon, especially during the winter. They ate oysters, clams, and lobster during the summer and fall.

The Nez Perce lived along the Snake River and its tributaries in Idaho, Oregon, and Washington. Each fall, the children went with their families to dig camas roots, which resemble potatoes. The roots were eaten fresh and were also stored for winter. Fresh greens were always collected in the spring. Nuts, berries, and fruit were plentiful in most areas in the fall.

Pemmican was a nutritious, high-protein food men

A NORTHWEST COAST FAMILY EATS A MEAL OF SALMON FROM WOODEN BOWLS.

took on hunting expeditions. It was made by pounding together dried meat, cornmeal, berries, and animal fat. Then it was rolled into a tight ball and wrapped in an animal skin. It lasted a very long time, because it did not need to be kept cold. Young boys looked forward to the time when they would be hunters and have their own supply of pemmican. Indulgent mothers let them taste it when they helped with its preparation.

Children from farming tribes ate lots of corn on the cob, ground cornmeal pancakes, and cornmeal mixed with meat and fish in a stew. They ate fresh beans and squash in summer and dried vegetables in winter.

A favorite corn dish was griddle cakes. Here is a typical recipe:

> 2 cups Indian meal (cornmeal)
> 1 cup flour
> 1 tablespoon dark molasses
> 1 teaspoon saleratus (baking soda)
> Add enough buttermilk or sour milk to make a stiff batter.

(Sour milk can be made by adding a teaspoon of vinegar to a cup of whole milk.) Mix everything together and drop by spoonfuls onto a hot griddle. Serve with butter and maple syrup.

SCHOOLS
without WALLS

Did children go to school?

Indian children woke up every morning in a classroom—their home. They went outdoors to another
classroom—the world around them. There was no such
thing as a school for Indian children. Learning and
playing were the same thing.

When children were five or six years old, they were
expected to practice the skills necessary to survive in
the adult world. The easiest way to do this was to imitate what their parents and elders were doing.

Who were their teachers?

Grandparents were the greatest source of informa-
tion and help, because they had the most free time.
Boys learned from the men of the tribe, and girls
learned from the women. Some boys enjoyed a spe-

17

**DELAWARE CHILDREN LEARN FROM THEIR
PARENTS AT HOME.**

cial relationship with an uncle, often one of their
mother's brothers, who taught them to fish and hunt
and brought them special gifts.

Girls learned from their mothers, grandmothers,
aunts, and older sisters, and frequently enjoyed a special friendship with one of their mother's sisters.

What did they learn?

The most important part of an Indian boy's education was learning to become a successful fisherman and
hunter. Boys were never expected to do women's
work. Instead they were encouraged to fish and hunt,
using small spears, slings, and arrows. Boys also
practiced shooting with slingshots made of leather
strips or pieces of flexible wood and bark.

In the Northeast, boys became adept at walking in
snowshoes, because hunting in winter was an important part of winter activity. Small snowshoes were
made for them when they were six years old.

**YOUNGSTERS IN THE NORTHEAST LEARN
TO WALK IN SHOWSHOES.**

Boys were urged to practice running and dodging, to use a shield to protect themselves from flying arrows and spears, and to ride a pony. They were made tough by taking daily baths in ice-cold water and by a rigid diet of very small quantities of corn and venison mixed with wild herbs.

Boys enjoyed a great deal more freedom than girls, because they could leave the campsite whenever they wished to practice their fishing and hunting skills. Beyond the eyes of parents, it was natural to play chase in the woods and to swim instead of fish.

**AN APACHE GIRL RIDES HORSEBACK
WITH HER UNCLE.**

A YOUNG GIRL COILS A CLAY POT.

**A YOUNG GIRL LEARNS HOW
TO SCRAPE A BUFFALO HIDE.**

**A MENOMINEE GIRL LEARNS
HOW TO SET A SNARE TRAP.**

Young girls were put to work helping the women of the tribe when they were five or six years of age, because women did all the work in and around the home. Girls helped to gather and prepare food, to harvest crops, and to ready them for winter storage. They learned how to remove the fur and soften the hides of animals, and to make clothing, robes, and coverings from the prepared skins. They learned to make clay pots, to weave baskets, and to build and furnish a comfortable dwelling for the family.

On the Great Plains, a man's job was done when a buffalo was killed. The women of the tribe went out into the prairie to slaughter it and bring the meat, bones, hide, and other useful materials back to camp.

Girls were left to care for younger brothers and sisters, even though they were not always able to make them behave. A rebellious young girl was once heard to threaten her mother, "I will drop this baby on its head, if it is not taken from me soon."

Young girls were encouraged to be as skillful in sports as boys. Often they became expert swimmers, because their mothers let them swim in the lake in exchange for doing the family laundry. Apache girls, who lived in New Mexico, Arizona, and Texas, learned to ride horseback when they were only six years old. Chippewa girls were trained to set fishnets when they were eight. Eventually, they also learned to haul in the nets and prepare the fish for storage. When Chippewa girls were eighteen years old, they went trapping with their fathers.

Menominee girls, who lived near Michigan and Wisconsin, were praised for their male attributes and learned to participate in many male activities. Women who could fish, hunt, race, and dance well were highly prized as wives and were greatly respected by everyone.

Children learned to keep themselves clean by bathing every day, summer and winter. There was no such thing as hot water for bathing, so they learned to tolerate cold water. In the Southwest, where water is very precious, children rubbed themselves all over each morning with clean sand.

Did they learn to read and write?

The Indians did not have a written language. Instead they drew pictures of important scenes and events on rock walls, bark roles, and on their tipi cov-

CHIPPEWA ENGRAVED BIRCHBARK SCROLL

IROQUOIS WAMPUM BELT

HOPI ROCK PAINTING

PLAINS PAINTED BUCKSKIN TIPI

**WAYS IN WHICH INDIAN TRIBES RECORDED
EVENTS AND TRADITIONS.**

ers. Tribes of the Chippewa kept records on sheets of birchbark which were taken out and read every fifteen years. If the bark showed decay, its contents was copied onto a fresh piece. The bark records told of the ancient forms of worship and instructed men in the right paths to follow.

Tribes of the Iroquois wove belts and robes out of shell, or wampum. These were created to carry messages from one tribe to another and to record historic events. Special designs were woven with purple and white wampum for different occasions. One man was put in charge of the belts, and each year he read the stories on them to other members of the tribe to refresh their memories. Young boys went with their fathers to listen when the belts were being read.

It was very important to watch and listen carefully all the time, because everyone had to rely on memory. The Indians listened to songs sung by women and stories told by elder tribesmen. The songs and stories were about folk heroes who succeeded or failed in their adventures depending on how well they obeyed tribal law. Children learned from the stories how to behave and the penalties for misbehavior. They learned to watch and listen to the wild animals, who also had souls worthy of consideration. They learned about the mysteries of the sun, moon, wind, and rain, and about the bountiful crops of mother earth. They learned the importance of getting along with others in a world where survival was often a joint effort.

Story-telling was a popular pastime, especially on winter nights. Old folks told stories that drew on memories, myths, fables, and adventures.

In northeastern Nebraska, children of the Omaha tribe learned about the pygmies—little people who hid in the woods and on the prairies, and led people astray. Other children believed the pygmies were responsible

TRIBAL CHIEF ACTS OUT AN
ADVENTURE STORY FOR
CHILDREN.

for creating cliffs and caves and for carving the rocks into strange shapes.

Children of the Northeast learned their history from tales that revolved around a culture hero called Nanabozho, who brought the Indians gifts of tobacco, meat, and corn, but who played tricks on them as well. Stories about Nanabozho taught children how important it was to be honest and trustworthy.

Often the tribal chief gathered children around him to tell them tales of his hunting and trapping adventures. If he was an especially good storyteller, he acted out his stories. Children learned from them where animals lived, how they got around, and how they might be outsmarted by a wise hunter. The chief also told wild tales about how he caught wolves or land otters with his bare hands. Children didn't learn from those stories, but they loved the humor and excitement.

Some tribes had official storytellers, who were in great demand at social events and enjoyed reputations as teachers. Storytellers acted out stories and included many vivid details. Children were encouraged to act out the stories they heard and to sing tribal songs. Sometimes shy boys were able to gain self-confidence by hiding behind masks when they danced. The masks disguised their faces, and they were able to be more sociable.

Were they religious?

Religion was a part of everyday life. Stories about how the earth was formed and how animals and people came into being were an important part of learning. Children were taught that things on earth were bound together and dependent upon one another. They learned to worship the land and everything it contained. They worshipped the forces of nature—the sun, the wind, and the rain. Their religious ceremonies did not mark events in time. Instead, they celebrated places on earth that were important to the Indian people such as a mountain, a lake, or a valley. The Indians believed animals, including reptiles and birds, were also people—just like the tribes. Plains Indians considered the buffalo a distinct "people," and tribe members of the Northwest Coast considered the salmon a distinct "people."

Spirits played an important role in everyday life, because they helped to connect the earth with the cosmos. They also helped to explain unnatural events such as hurricanes, which might be blamed on an angry spirit. A bountiful crop, on the other hand, might be attributed to a generous spirit. Indian people appealed to the spirits for assistance when they needed it. A shaman, or priest, was often called upon to convince a spirit to help. Indian people knew a great deal about nature, but they believed a job was well done only when the spirits had been properly thanked. For example, they planted corn and fertilized the soil at exactly the right time of year. Yet, they held dances and festivals to encourage the rain and sun spirits to make their crops grow. To the Indian people, these dances and festivals were as important as the fertilizer.

Did they practice medicine?

Medicine and religion were closely intertwined, so it was natural for children to learn which plants cured particular illnesses and how to prepare them. There were numerous herbal cures which children learned while growing up. For example, the tribes of the Iroquois boiled wild geranium roots *(geranium maculatum)* to make tea, which they drank to cure mouth sores. Geranium roots contain tannin, which is a very good medicine for drying wounds and sores.

Disease was often believed to occur because a person was out of harmony with the earth, or because the person did something that was forbidden by tribal ethics. Medicine men and shamans were thought to be in better contact with the spirits and could get power from dreams. Dreams were a good way to contact the supernatural. Besides being in possession of powerful medicines, medicine men talked to the spirits and acted as intermediaries between the sick person and the spirit.

FAMILIES
LARGE and SMALL

How many brothers and sisters?

Indian families were never very large. The basic family unit usually consisted of a mother, a father, two children, and two grandparents. Because there were no modern-day medicines or hospitals, Indian women often died giving birth, and many children died when they were quite young.

Who lived in the house?

Besides the basic family unit, there was often a larger, or extended, family which included adopted children, the wife's unmarried sisters, and additional wives.

Children were adopted by another family if their own parents died, or if they had been captured from an enemy tribe. They were treated with love and affection,

like any other member of the family, and grew to be
loyal tribal members.

Indian families worked and played together all year
round. They shared happy times and helped one another in time of need.

What are clans and tribes?

Beyond the extended family unit, there were larger
groups called clans. Clans were a convenient way for
Indian people to organize family property and give
family members responsibilities and duties. A clan
consisted of all the father's or all the mother's blood
relatives. Men and women of the same clan could not
marry each other, but had to marry outside their clan.
Even though a man moved in with his wife's clan after
marriage, he did not join her clan, but continued to
obey the rules and traditions of his own people. Among
families of the Southwest, where Indian people lived
in permanent-type villages, a husband often spent more
time in his mother's home than he did in his own
home. Children are automatically members of their
mother's clan when they are born. This explains the
close relationships developed with the mother's brothers and sisters.

We often think of a tribe as a small group of Indian
people who have one chief and speak the same language. This is only partly true. A true tribe is a very
large group of Indian people who speak the same language, but who are seldom organized with a leader.
Most of the time, small local groups are called tribes.
In the Northeast for example, the Abnaki, Penobscot,
and Passamquoddy Indians of Maine; the Massachus-
set Indians who lived around Boston; the Narraganset
Indians of Rhode Island; and the Mahican Indians of
New York, are all considered tribes because each

group had a leader; yet they all spoke the Algonquian language.

What kinds of houses?

Long ago Indian children lived in many different kinds of houses. Houses, which were built of natural materials—wood, mud, skins, twigs, and stone—had different shapes, depending upon where they were located, how they were used, and what materials could be found.

In many regions, homes were built to hold several families. Wigwams, tipis, grass- and earth-covered dwellings were usually designed to accommodate one to six families, while the adobe and mudbrick houses of the Southwest, the longhouses of the Iroquois, and the plankhouses of the Northwest Coast Indians held many families. When a house was shared, it was usually by sisters and their families or members of their clan.

Iroquois longhouses were supported by long poles and covered with bark, while Northwest coast plankhouses were built of long cedar boards. Both types were long and narrow, from fifty to one hundred fifty feet long and eighteen feet wide. In the center, each family had a firepit surrounded by low benches, separating each family's space. Children on the Northwest coast left their plankhouses in summer and moved with their families to a favorite fishing site, which might also be shared with clansmen.

Adobe houses, often called puebloes, were sectioned off into rooms, and families were given space with their own clan. There were stone or adobe benches around the walls of each room, and a corner was left vacant for a corn-grinding trough. Niches, built into the side of the walls, held baskets and cooking pots.

In wigwams and earthen lodges, families created private spaces by placing a pole across the dwelling and hanging a woven mat as a curtain. Roundhouses sometimes had only one shared firepit.

Almost all Indian houses had wood or stone benches along the outside walls for sitting and sleeping. Household possessions and children's toys were stored under the benches.

Of course, all tribes built shelters at their seasonal hunting and fishing sites, but usually these were large enough only for one family. In warm weather, families preferred to live outdoors and use the dwelling for

AN INDIAN FAMILY WORKS AND PLAYS TOGETHER.

storing their belongings and for sleeping on rainy nights.

What were the house rules?

House rules were very similar for all Indian children. Inside the home they played in their own space and did not go into another family's area. Toys had to be picked up after play. If not, they were thrown away, and parents would not allow them to be replaced for a very long time.

Grandmothers occupied the most important seat in the house, but mothers made and enforced the house rules. As one entered a wigwam or tent, the grand-

PLAINS PLATEAU ALASKA

PLAINS EARTHLODGE

SOUTHEAST

NORTHEAST LONGHOUSES

SOUTHWEST

INDIAN HOMES WERE MADE OF WOOD, MUD, SKINS, TWIGS, AND STONE.

mother was seated on the right—the place of honor—with her husband and sons seated behind her. On the left side of the wigwam, her daughter sat with her young children and her husband. Guests were always seated opposite the entrance.

Grandfathers were masters of ceremonies at home, and husbands spoke only in their absence. Everyone else gave visitors only the slightest form of greeting. If the husband and grandfather were gone at the same time, the grandmother became spokesperson for the family. In her absence, the woman of the house spoke to the visitor. Young girls always remained silent when a guest appeared and no men were at home.

NORTHWEST COAST PLANKHOUSE
MADE OF CEDAR BOARDS

PUEBLO OF THE
SOUTHWEST
MADE OF ADOBE

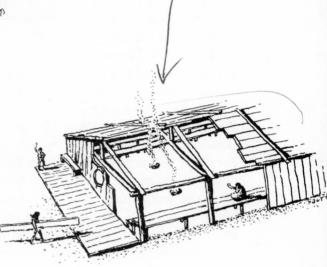

PLAINS EARTHLODGE FRAMED OF
TIMBER AND COVERED WITH SOD

The customary joking, laughing, and energetic play of an Indian family were suspended when guests appeared. Children were expected to sit up straight and remain quiet. Giggling was strictly forbidden in front of company.

Children learned when they were very young that it was important to behave while eating. It was never bad manners to eat with their fingers, especially when food was cooked directly over the fire and served in large chunks. Stew was a popular Indian dish and was usually eaten with a spoon, the only eating utensil available. The meat was cut beforehand with a sharp bone, a shell, or a stone knife. In most Indian homes, the stewpot stayed over the fire all day, and family members ate whenever they were hungry. Women used a large ladle, made of wood or horn, to scoop the stew from the pot into individual bowls. Each family member had a bowl made of clay, wood, or shell and a small spoon made of wood or horn. When spoons were not available, stew was eaten by tipping the bowl to the mouth. Some tribes used tightly woven baskets for bowls.

An Apache child was taught never to grab food or drink, and to wait before eating until all the older people were served.

In northern California, a Yurok child caught eating too fast had the food taken away and was sent outside. A child had to use very good manners when guests were present. Guests were always offered food when they came to visit. A mother served her guests first, then her husband, and then her mother. Children were served according to age, the oldest first. A mother always served herself last. After the meal, the guests left the table first, followed by the husband. Children stayed seated until the mother had cleaned the bowls and spoons and swept the floor.

TOYS and GAMES for PLAYTIME

Did boys and girls play together?

Boys and girls in some regions did not play together after they were five or six years old, because the skills they had to learn were quite different. Men spent most of their time on fishing and hiking expeditions, and women stayed behind tending gardens and running the home. Young girls stayed with the women of the tribe to help. Young boys, on the other hand, did not go with their fathers, but were expected to practice hunting and fishing skills. Like their fathers, they were free to leave the village for as long as they liked. If children were not kept separate, they would not learn the skills of their own sex.

Some parents went to a great deal of effort to keep boys and girls apart. In western Montana and Idaho, Salish girls traveled a distance each day to a miniature village built for them by the women of the tribe. They learned to twine mats and bags, to do beadwork and embroidery. Girls loved to play house and enjoyed the special attention given to them by the older women. Doting grandmothers lavished praise when the girls mastered difficult skills, and sometimes hung their handiwork from a tree branch in the village for everyone to admire.

On the Great Plains, where tribes followed migrating herds of buffalo, boys and girls spent the days together in play villages until they were ten or twelve years old. When the family made camp, the girls put up small skin-covered tipis, large enough to crawl inside. Boys and girls imitated the activities of their parents in these pretend villages. Omaha girls made tipi poles of tall, tough sunflower stalks, which they covered with skin robes. Boys often went home and asked their mothers for food, then they presented it to the girls as if they'd obtained it themselves. Girls of the Gros Ventre tribe, who lived in northern Montana, demanded that the boys hunt buffalo. The boys would leave the play area and return a short time later neighing like horses returning from a successful hunt. Girls would meet the hunters and exclaim, "Oh, you brought back all this meat!" Then they pretended to cut it up for cooking.

Sometimes boys actually succeeded in tracking down a stray buffalo calf, a small gopher, or another animal for the girls. Then they had a regular adultlike festival. If there was leftover meat, the children proudly presented it to their parents when they returned home for the night.

Young boys liked to pretend they were ponies, getting down on all four limbs outside a girl's tipi. Girls treated the ponies like their own, loading them down with tipi poles and household possessions as if it were time to move camp. Then the boys entertained the girls by being particularly rambunctious and dragging the toys through the brush or into streams. The girls ran behind, wailing and shouting. At other times, the ponies acted docile, trotting along beside the girls, obeying their commands.

Boys also delighted in showing off their racing skills. They staged mock horseraces for the girls, dragging large sunflower stalks between their legs like hobby horses.

When they got bored playing house, they staged make-believe battles with toy weapons. Girls slapped mud on their legs to represent blood and went away weeping. Dead bodies were prepared in the proper fashion by wrapping them in blankets. Some girls even wrapped large buffalo legs in blankets pretending they held a frightened child.

What kinds of toys did they have?

Indian children owned a variety of toys, because parents wanted to make sure they used authentic implements when they played house and went hunting. Parents and grandparents enjoyed making toys for children. Boys were given bows and arrows and bone knives for male tasks, while girls were given tiny baskets and pots suitable for their miniature homes.

Girls played with dolls made of wood, bark, grass cloth, cornhusks, and corncobs. On the western coast of Vancouver Island in British Columbia, Nootka girls dressed up clam shells with strips of rags and set them in rows in the sand so they looked like children. Salish girls made dolls with stick bodies and clay or pebble heads. They dressed the dolls in grass or buckskin. Girls also played with tiny clay dishes and pots. Grandmothers made miniature bowls, dippers, cups, and jars for their granddaughters. They decorated the

AN INDIAN FAMILY SITS IN THE
WIGWAM IN TRADITIONAL
LOCATIONS.

pottery and fired it in the family kiln. Hopi girls played with tiny water canteens like those used to bring water to the tops of the mesas, where they lived, from the springs below. They also practiced corn grinding, using bits of sand because corn was too precious to waste. The make-believe corn was cooked in small clay dishes. Girls also had dishes made of horn and wood as well as little baskets of willow and bags made of skin.

Chippewa girls strung berries together to make necklaces and wove pine needles into interesting designs to hang around their necks. They played with

RAMBUNCTIOUS BOYS DRAG A TRAVOIS THROUGH THE CHILDREN'S CAMPSITE.

dolls made of basswood leaves, pine needles, and grass tied together with fine pieces of bark. Pine needle dolls were made to dance by standing them in a container of water and shaking it back and forth.

In Florida, Seminole girls made dolls from the brown portion of the palmetto leaf. They dressed the dolls in brightly colored cotton cloth, leaving only the head showing.

Boys were given toy bows and arrows as soon as they could walk. Fathers, grandfathers, and uncles continued to make larger pieces of gear for the boys as they grew. Boys practiced shooting with toy sling-

LEARNING TO HOLD A SMALL BOW AND AIM A BLUNT ARROW.

A TOY KNIFE WITH A FLAKED STONE BLADE

shots, bean shooters, and flipping sticks. They were never allowed to aim a toy weapon at another person or a pet. If they did, they were sternly disciplined and the toy was taken away.

Boys were always given a target to shoot at. Sometimes the target was a life-size bark cutout set in the snow and made to look like a moose or deer. Men went with boys into the woods to help them look for the targets.

Children living along the northwestern shore of the St. Lawrence River practiced target shooting each spring while their fathers watched. It was believed fathers would enjoy a prosperous hunting season if their sons showed skill at shooting down targets.

Some boys practiced with slingshots made of leather strips or of pieces of flexible wood and bark. Salish boys made slingshots of leather. They attached a string to one end of the leather and wrapped a pebble in the string. Then they whirled the slingshot over their heads, and the pebble flew through the air.

Similarly, Nootka boys took a ten-inch strip of flexible cedar and bent it in two. They put a pebble against one end of the strip and, when they released it, the pebble flew through the air with great speed and accuracy.

In northern California, Pomo youths stuck flexible twigs in the ground, held a stone against the free end, and bent the twig backwards. When the twig was released, the stone went flying toward its target.

Hopi boys, living in northeastern Arizona, and Zuni boys, who lived southwest of Gallup, New Mexico, made bean shooters of sunflower stalks, while Nootka boys made them of long lengths of kelp, a strong tuberous seaweed found along the Pacific shore. Bits of wood and tiny pebbles were shot through bean shooters.

CHIPPEWA GIRL HOLDS A PINE NEEDLE DOLL AND A LEAF DOLL.

A YOUNG MAN SHOOTS AT A MOOSE TARGET.

Indian boys, who lived in the mountains of northern Mexico, carved animal hooves on the bottom of thick branches, then pressed the carving into the ground to give the impression that animals were about. Sometimes they carved footprints into thick pieces of pine bark and strapped the bark to their feet like a pair of sandals. With the carved portion pressing into the ground, the boys ran and walked like the animal they were trying to imitate.

What kinds of games did they play?

Indian people loved ball games of all kinds. They made balls out of every conceivable natural material—wood, stone, animal skin, animal bladders, bark, or grass softly woven into circles. Some people say that the moon is a ball which was thrown against the sky in a game a long time ago. Many games the Indians gave us are still played today—lacrosse, skinny (played like field hockey), football, and bowling, to name a few. Team games were as popular then as they are now. Sometimes a team was all boys, but at other times it could be all girls.

Lacrosse was played much the same as it is today. A ball, made of deer hide, was thrown into the air and team members were expected to keep it from their opponents' goal by running across the field flinging the ball through the air or carrying it in a special long-handled racquet. The game developed teamwork and running skills.

GIRLS PLAY LACROSSE IN CANOES.

Girls played lacrosse in canoes. The ball was twice as large as that used on land, but it was much lighter. The throwing sticks were longer and lighter, and basket hoops were larger. Ten to twenty girls played the game with a paddler and a thrower in each canoe. It was a wonderful summer game, and the girls prepared themselves to be dumped overboard into the water.

Boys played a game called javelin, or net hoop, in which a large hoop, divided into sections, was rolled over flat ground for one hundred and fifty feet. Players tried to pierce the hoop with darts as it moved. This game was a good test of eyesight, fleetness, and the ability to throw.

Another game for boys was called snow snake and was played only in winter. The snake—a long flattened rod with one end rounded and the other notched as a finger grip—was thrown over the snow to see how far it would go. A peg was stuck into the snow to indicate where each snake had stopped. Sometimes a log was dragged through the snow to make a track for throwing.

Girls played both hand ball and foot ball. Balls were often made of animal bladders filled with antelope hair. Occasionally the outside of a ball was covered with a woven netting to make it last longer. Women also played double ball. Two balls of clay, or sand, were covered with buckskin and held together with a long thong. The object of the game was to lift the weighted

A BOY THROWS A SNAKE OVER THE SNOW.

balls by the thong with a long stick and pass them along the field to other players, who kept the balls moving until they could be thrown over a goal pole at the end of the field.

Skinny was a game played by both girls and boys and sometimes with mixed teams. Like our field hockey, the object of the game was to drive a ball along the ground or through the air into the opponents' goal. The opponents' job was to defend their goal. Skinny balls were about the size of a baseball, but softer.

Children were discouraged from gambling or playing games of chance like those enjoyed by their parents. Instead they played with tops, one of a child's most prized possessions. The top, an inverted cone made to spin with a string or a stick, was made of wood, hide, horn, stone, or clay. Some tops were painted in bright colors and ornamented with feathers and hair. Although they were generally considered a boy's toy, some girls had their own tops.

In the Northeast, children sat in a circle while one child spun a top in the center of the circle. The twirler asked a series of questions that were answered by the direction the top pointed when it stopped spinning. For example, "Where will meat come from this winter?" If the top pointed north, hunting would be best in that direction. If it pointed west, they believed hunters would have more success if they traveled west to look for game.

Another game focused on personal questions such as "Whose mother can dance best?" or "Who will marry first?" The spinning top fell and pointed to the lucky winner.

Some Indian children spun tops in an effort to bring the wind or to find its direction.

Indian and Eskimo children living in the Subarctic shared their tops or used them in groups. Children sat in circles and took turns spinning a top to see who could get it going and keep it going the longest. One person would start the top spinning, then run out the door and all the way around the house to see if he could get back before it stopped spinning. If more than one person made it back, the spinning and running continued until all but one child was eliminated.

**BOYS IN THE NORTHERN PLAINS SPIN
A TOP ON THE ICE.**

Children living in the northern Great Plains and in southern Canada reserved top spinning only for the winter months, when tops could be spun across the glassy ice of lakes and ponds. Cheyenne boys, living in Montana and Oklahoma, believed hair would grow on their bodies if they played with tops in summer. Since Indian men grew very little body hair, young boys feared they would have to have the hair removed with tweezers. To insure that no tops were used in summer, some children threw them in the water in spring when the ice was beginning to melt.

Children living on the Great Plains had tops made of buffalo horn or carved from oak and cedar wood. They twirled their tops on a smooth surface and whipped them with a stick to keep them going.

Near the Black Hills of South Dakota, Oglala boys spun tops in the center of a square outlined in the dirt. The top had to stay within the square the entire time it was spinning in order to win the game.

Children also played with a simple whirling toy called a buzz. Buzzes were made by drilling two holes in a small round piece of wood, bone, pottery, stone, shell, or gourd. Children strung cord through the holes and tied it together. The buzz was centered on the cord, which was stretched between both hands. Then it was twirled forward until it became tightly wrapped. By moving the hands in and out toward each other, alternately tightening and loosening the cord, the buzz was made to whirl.

Children in the Northeast, California, and on the Great Plains made buzzes of buffalo and deer toe bones. They twirled them on rawhide thongs or on long thin pieces of sinew. Sometimes they made wood handles which they attached to the ends of the cords. Hopi children made clay buzzes, which they twirled on soft cotton cordage.

When children did not play with toys or play games with their friends, it was considered a bad sign for the coming season.

BECOMING an ADULT

How did children prepare for adulthood?

Indian boys and girls left behind their carefree years of "learning while playing" when they were between ten and twelve years of age. Then they were initiated into adulthood with elaborate rituals, week-long religious ceremonies, and public announcements. It was like a combination bar mitzvah/graduation exercise.

Children enjoyed the attention they were given during their initiation ceremonies. It was a time of anticipation and excitement and, for most Indian children, a deeply religious experience.

Tribes shared common beliefs, but their rituals, taboos, and ceremonies varied. Some rituals were painful and frightening, but children had learned long before they came of age that pain and fear were a part of life. They were told, "If you take an interest in fasting and are not afraid, you will be prepared for your initiation ceremony."

A YOUNG GIRL ENTERS A MENSTRUAL LODGE.

Indian children did not go to church, just as they did
not go to school, because their life was their religion.
They worshipped nature and the mysteries of the uni-
verse as part of their daily lives. They knew that religion was very personal and should be conducted in
private. They talked to the spirits whenever they
needed to, just as their parents did.

Young girls were plunged into adulthood as soon as
they experienced their first menstrual period. Older
women of the tribe whisked them off to an isolated hut
where they stayed for at least four days. Women kept
watch over them day and night because it was believed everything they did at this time influenced their
entire lives. Some tribes believed they were also
charged at this time with power dangerous to men.

Girls spent the daylight hours learning everything
they needed to know to become women. They were
instructed in the proper way to behave and were tested
on their womanly skills. Many tribes forbade women
from scratching their heads with their fingernails during isolation, because the head was the most important part of the body. Instead they used a long stick.
Others believed it was harmful to allow water to touch

the lips at this time. Tribes of the Tlingit, who lived along the southeastern coast of Alaska, made young women drink water through the wing bone of a white-headed eagle.

Girls living in the region of southern California were made to swallow balls of tobacco as part of their ceremony. Then they had to lie down in a pit filled with hot rocks. They were covered with another layer of rocks and made to remain there for three days. At night, men danced around them and during the day women danced. The girls were allowed to get up each day when the rocks were reheated. While they were up, they could have a very small bit of food. At the end of three days, the wife of the village chief painted the girl's face and body. Sometimes the girls were also tattooed, which is a more permanent kind of painting.

Apache girls took part in a four-day ceremony in which shamans sang songs, masked dancers performed at night to bring girls supernatural blessings, and women worked tirelessly all day instructing the girls in proper behavior. In summer, when the girls were honored at a big celebration, they were often required to dance up and down in place facing the sun for two or three hours, wearing heavy beaded buckskin dresses. This was a test of endurance and was often extremely difficult.

Tribes of the Great Plains secluded young girls for four nights in a small tipi and kept them under the supervision of an old woman. During this time, they were expected to have a vision, something most tribes required only of young men.

Visions occur when a person is awake and differ from dreams which occur during sleep. Girls were encouraged to have a vision while they chopped wood, sewed, or listened to the older women. They were given very little food to eat and on the fourth night,

**A YOUNG BOY LYING IN A PIT HAS A SUCCESSFUL
VISION QUEST.**

other women came to pray for them. After the pray-
ers, the women piled up the girl's chopped wood, cer-
emonially pushed it over, and then took it home. Girls
went home, and their parents threw a big party in
which guests were given gifts.

A few wealthy tribes living in the Pacific Northwest
created their own customs because they owned slaves.
Young girls did not have to work, because there was
always help in the house and their initiation didn't fo-
cus on their womanly skills. Instead they were made
to stay in a small room in the plankhouse, away from
everyone else, for two to three years. Their seclusion
did not always occur with their first menses, but could
occur earlier. The girls did nothing during the day and
emerged only at night in secret with their mothers. The
inactivity and tight quarters in which they lived made
them weak and often slightly crippled. These defects,
however, were highly valued, because they were proof
the girl came from an extremely important family. In

addition, the years of isolation made them mysterious characters who were sought after by young men when they came out.

Girls living on the Great Plains were given parties to celebrate their ability to marry. They suddenly became less playful and stayed around camp. During this time, young men strolled through the villages looking at the girls, who were closely watched by parents and relatives. If a man was interested in a young woman, he talked to her father or brother to get to know the family. Girls living on the Plains were actively pursued by interested young men and did not have to marry a man chosen by their parents.

Among tribes of the Iroquois, girls told their mothers the name of the man they wanted to marry, and the mother became friendly with the young man's mother. If both mothers agreed, the girl cooked bread and hung it on the young man's door. It was agreed that if the young man lived after eating the bread, they could marry.

Hopi girls did not make a fuss about becoming adults. There were no celebrations, no fasting, and no separation from the rest of the tribe. Instead the girls just quietly changed their hairstyle to show they were now marriageable.

A HOPI GIRL INDICATES SHE HAS MARRIED BY CHANGING HER HAIRSTYLE.

Isolation and painful rituals were almost always followed by public celebrations where girls emerged as women. Many tribes held festivals for young women, and people danced and sang with joy for long periods of time.

What is a vision quest?

Becoming an adult was almost always more difficult for boys, and there were few celebrations held in honor of manhood. Most boys were expected to go on a vision quest, which meant taking a trip into the mountains alone, or far from home, and fasting until they had a vision. The vision could take the form of any spirit: a human, a wild animal, the wind, the rain, or the sun. Whatever the vision, it had to give the boy direction for the rest of his life. The spirit he saw would become his guardian spirit and remain with him forever.

Among tribes of the Winnebego, who lived in the area of Green Bay, Wisconsin, and their neighbors, the Chippewa, men and women encouraged a boy to seek a guardian spirit from the time he was seven years old. A boy went to seek a vision when he felt the time was right. There was, however, no pressure to be successful until he was at least twelve years of age. Early attempts were undoubtedly good practice.

Boys fasted during their quest, hoping the spirits would pity them and hurry up a vision. Sometimes they even cut off a finger or stuck bone pins into their flesh and hung weights on the pins to stretch and pull it. For some young men, fasting was a way to remove the "smell" of the common world, which was always less pure than the spiritual world.

When boys went off to have a vision, their parents told them where to go and exactly what route to take.

They learned all about the land over which they would travel so they would not get lost or be scared.

For young men living on the Great Plains, buffalo were a popular form for a spirit in a vision, although elks, eagles, and sparrow hawks would do. Some tribes chose to see their guardian spirits in dogs and rabbits. For many young men, spirits appeared in the form of distorted human beings, who hinted at what they were but did not reveal themselves. Young men, who were members of the Pawnee tribes, sometimes saw spirits in the form of stars, the moon, or the sun.

The Pawnee people of Oklahoma have a legend that tells about the mosquito guardian spirit that enabled a young man to become chief of his tribe. The mosquito was acceptable to the tribe's elders, because a guardian spirit could appear in any form.

Tribes of the Crow, who lived in southwestern Montana and northern Wyoming, believed a spirit could tell boys how to become warriors and dress for war, or could give them medicine bags to make them medicine men. A guardian spirit could forbid boys from eating particular foods and might instruct them on proper behavior. If boys went against their guardian spirit, they might lose it or find their lives in danger. Boys who belonged to the Crow tribes, living along the Missouri River, were believed to be adopted by their guardian spirits.

A boy living on the Great Plains might sometimes ask one of the old men of his tribe to go with him on his vision quest. The two went to a lonely spot and dug a pit. The boy got in and the older man covered him with branches. The boy fasted in the pit for four days, and the old man checked on him each day. It was common to have a vision of an animal important to the people of the tribe. If the boy had a successful vision, he often took as his own name that of the animal he saw.

Hopi boys had very mild initiation rites. They took sweatbaths with the men of the tribe. Sweathouses were small wooden structures just large enough to hold four or five seated men, whose heads stuck out the top. A sweathouse contained hot rocks upon which water was dripped to produce very hot steam. Men liked relaxing and socializing in sweathouses. When they got out, they enjoyed scraping their bodies with long, flat animal-bone scrapers to clean themselves. Boys were invited to go on important hunting trips with men of the tribe during their initiation. Both these experiences were believed to influence a young man's future.

Some tribes initiated young boys into secret societies at the same time they were initiated into adulthood.

Tribes of California did not want to take a chance that young boys would not receive a vision, so they gave them the juice from a wild plant to induce hallucination and create a vision.

Perhaps the most painful ceremonies for young boys were those of the Algonkian tribes living near Ottawa and Quebec. Their ceremonies were designed to symbolize the death of a boy and the birth of a man. Young boys were beaten by older men of the tribe while women, especially their mothers, wept as if they were being killed. Then the boys were painted white and put in shallow pits overnight while men sang and performed rituals over them. The next day, the boys were taken into the woods by an elder tribesman, who instructed them in sacred customs. When the boys returned to the village, they were no longer boys, but men.

All aspects of a vision quest were sacred. Men of the Sioux tribe, who moved from Minnesota and Wisconsin onto the Great Plains during the eighteenth century, learned to open their medicine bundles in private and to reserve sacred songs for medicine men and sachems, or chiefs. Children learned that spirits could be good and helpful, but that they could also hurt and punish. For this reason, sacred objects such as medicine bundles and songs sung during initiation ceremonies were treated with great respect and reverence.

If young men could not achieve visions, they continued to try. If after a long period of time they were not successful, they could buy power from a more fortunate, powerful man. The purchaser learned the sacred songs and taboos of the spirit he now shared. However, on the Great Plains, visions could not be sold, and men who failed to have their own guardian spirit were considered failures.

Dreams and visions were important throughout the lives of Indian boys and girls and played a major role in all their activities. Men were always in quest of some sort of vision, but none was as important as that of their initiation into adulthood.

When did they marry?

Girls and boys were ready to be married by the time they were fifteen years old. Courtship customs varied from tribe to tribe, but most marriages were arranged by the family or by the tribe. Getting married was not a cause for celebration, because it was not a religious occasion. Instead, it was considered a contract between two people or two families. It was important for a man to marry young and have a wife to make and mend clothes, weave baskets, scrape skins, carry home meat, build the house, and gather and prepare food. A women needed a man to protect her, to hunt and fish, and to father her children. Occasionally the wife's family hosted a small party to let friends and neighbors know a daughter had married. Newlyweds generally went to live with the wife's family for a year, or until their first child was born. Tribes of the Woodland often expected a new bridegroom to give his father-in-law all the animals he hunted. In exchange the boy was clothed, fed, and housed. Some tribes requested a bridegroom give gifts to the family of the girl he chose to marry. The bride's family often gave gifts in return, showing that both families accepted and approved the marriage.

INDIAN CHILDREN TODAY

How have they changed?

The lives of Indian children began to change when the first settlers came to their shores. The settlers had a long tradition of land ownership and set out to purchase as much land as possible. Not understanding the concept of land ownership, many Indian people signed papers that gave away their land. It wasn't long before Indian children began to feel hunger for the first time, because their families had nowhere to plant their gardens and men were driven from their traditional hunting and fishing sites.

Some tribes became angry at the settlers and tried to reclaim their land forcefully, but arrows and tomahawks were no match for guns, and many Indians died.

Eventually every Indian tribe in the New World was rounded up by the settlers and forced to live on reservations—land set aside for Indian people only. Reservation land was chosen because it appeared to be useless to the settlers.

The Indian people were expected to re-establish their way of life on these reservations, but that was not possible. Young men, who had been raised to hunt and fish, found no game, and fishnets and harpoons lay idle for want of freshwater lakes or streams. Young women, who had learned to prepare animal hides, could find no animals. Weaving material, suitable for traditional baskets, could not be found in the new and limited areas. Reservation life was especially difficult

CONTEMPORARY INDIAN CHILDREN LEARN HOW TO FLAKE STONE ARROWHEADS AND DO BEADWORK.

for children, because their parents were not practicing traditional customs. How could they play if there was no one to imitiate? Boys were not given small bows and arrows, because men did not want to frustrate them. And girls were not taught to weave small baskets, because weaving materials could not be found and, besides, iron pots were easy to come by. Mothers and grandmothers did not even make them corn, bark, or wooden dolls anymore. Instead, they made cloth dolls dressed like Indians to sell to children of the settlers.

Even the religious ceremonies and festivals from which Indian children learned their history were forbidden on the reservations. Indians caught practicing what was believed to be a religious ceremony were seriously punished. For a people whose religion is integral to their entire lives, this made life itself a punishment.

Reservations were run by non-Indians, who were given money by the government to help the Indian people learn how to live like the European settlers. Children were taken away from their homes and made to attend boarding schools off the reservations, away from their parents and clansmen. They were forbidden to speak their Indian languages and could not talk to anyone except in English. It is no wonder an unfair stereotype of the Indian developed which depicts Indian people as silent, speechless stonefaces who speak only in grunts. Adults as well as children did not dare speak in their native tongue for fear of punishment.

Children were mystified by the European concept of learning, which meant sitting on hard boards all day looking at "talking papers." The free, trusting lifestyle of an Indian child was replaced by a rigid, humorless form of discipline which frightened them. They missed the warm assurance of parents, grandparents, and elders, who corrected their mistakes with kindness and encouraged them with praise.

After much pleading by the Indians, the government finally agreed to build schools *on* the reservations. Even though Indian children still learned European culture in the schools, they could be with their beloved families each day.

Today, many Indian children still attend reservation schools, but now they are staffed with Indian teachers and administered by Indian people. Children living on small reservations are often bussed off the reservation to public schools each day.

On the Navajo reservation in Arizona and New Mexico, which is one of the largest, the tribe has built its own college. It offers two years of courses leading to an associate degree or a certificate of proficiency in a vocational field. There are also courses in the Navajo language and culture. For students who want to live at the school, there are dormitories, one of which is built in the form of a hogan, a particular type of dwelling favored by the Navajos.

Where do they live?

For almost two hundred years, the Indian people have struggled to make sense out of reservation life. They have tried unsuccessfully to straddle two very different cultures and have ended up living in extreme poverty. Their reservations are still overcrowded, and the land on which they live will never support a traditional Indian lifestyle. There is, however, a rebirth of awareness and concern by non-Indians, along with a rebirth of culture by the Indian people themselves. Indian children are now learning how to direct their own futures with renewed self-awareness.

Many Indians were not able to survive the extreme hardships of reservation life and moved away to be assimilated with the rest of the population. In fact, more than half of the Indian people today do not live on reservations, and Indian children share the activities, education, and traditions of the modern-day world. Like all other American children, they go to public schools by bus, play sports, and go to the movies. They also attend prep schools, colleges, and universities around the world. Chilocco Indian School in Oklahoma, Haskell Institute in Kansas, and the American Indian Arts Institute in New Mexico cater entirely to Indian students, some of whom go on to a four-year college.

Many American people try to preserve the customs of their parents and grandparents, some of which are based on religious beliefs. Similarly, the Indian people want to preserve their religion and customs, and are teaching their children the truth about their heritage. They do not wish to maintain an outdated lifestyle, even though other Americans, in retrospect, think it is interesting, unique, and valuable. Nor do they like to be spoken about in the past tense—as if they no longer exist. Their history is of the past, like all other histories but, today, the lives of many Indian families are no different than those of other Americans.

Suggested Reading

Ashabranner, Brent. *To Live in Two Worlds: American Indian Youth Today*. New York: Dodd Mead, 1984.

Gates, Frieda. *North American Indian Masks*. New York: Walker and Company, 1982.

Henry, Edna. *Native American Cookbook*. New York: Julian Messner, 1983.

Kazimizoff, Theordore L. *The Last Algonquin*. New York: Walker and Company, 1982.

Logan, Adelphena. *Memories of Sweet Grass*. Washington, Connecticut: American Indian Archaeological Institute, Inc., 1979.

Lyons, Grant. *Pacific Coast Indians of North America*. New York: Julian Messner, 1983.

Robinson, Gail. *Raven, the Trickster*. New York: Atheneum, 1982.

Siegel, Beatrice. *Indians of the Woodland: Before and After the Pilgrims*. New York: Walker and Company, 1972.

Simon, Nancy and Evelyn Wolfson. *American Indian Habitats*. New York: David McKay Co., Inc., 1978.

Wolfson, Evelyn. *American Indian Utensils*. New York: David McKay Co., Inc., 1979.

———. *American Indian Tools and Ornaments*. New York: David McKay Co., Inc., 1981.

Selected Bibliography

Copway, G. *The Traditional History and Sketches of the Ojibway Nation*. Toronto: Cole Publishing Co., 1972.

Culin, Stewart. *Games of the North American Indian*. New York: Dover, 1975.

Drucker, Philip. *Indians of the Northwest Coast*. New York: The Natural History Press, 1955.

Erdoes, Richard. *The Sun Dance People: The Plains Indians, Their Past and Present*. New York: Random House, 1972.

Favour, Edith. *Indian Games, Toys and Pastimes of Maine and the Maritimes*. The Robert Abee Museum, Bar Harbour, Maine, 1974.

Fletcher, Alice C. and Frances LaFlesche. *The Omaha Tribe*. Vol. II. Lincoln, Nebraska: University of Nebraska Press, 1972.

Garbarino, Merwyn S. *Native American Heritage*. Boston: Little Brown & Co., 1976.

Gates, Frieda. *North American Indian Masks*. New York: Walker and Company, 1982.

Gunther Erna. *Indian Life on the Northwest Coast*. Chicago: University of Chicago Press, 1972.

Helm, June, ed. *Handbook of North American Indians*, Vol. 6, *Subarctic*. Washington, D. C.: Smithsonian Institution, 1981.

Heizer, Robert F., ed. *Handbook of North American Indians*, Vol. 8, *California*. Washington, D. C.: Smithsonian Institution, 1978.

Highwater, Jamake. *Ritual of the Wind: North American Indian Ceremonies*. New York: Viking Press, 1977.

Kazimizoff, Theordore L. *The Last Algonquin*. New York: Walker and Company, 1982.

Loeb, Edwin Meyer. *Pomo Folkways*. Berkeley: University of California Press, 1926.

Lowie, Robert H. *Indians of the Plains*. New York: Natural History Press, 1954.

Morgan, Lewis H. *League of the Iroquois,* Vol. II. New York: Dodd Mead & Co., 1901.

Neithammer, Carolyn. *Daughters of the Earth: The Lives and Legends of American Indian Women*. New York: Collier Books, 1977.

Newcomb. W. W., Jr. *The Indians of Texas*. Austin, Texas: University of Texas Press, 1961.

Ritzenthaler, Robert E. and Pat Ritzenthaler. *The Woodland Indians of the Western Great Lakes*. New York: The Natural History Press, 1970.

Siegel, Beatrice. *Indians of the Woodland: Before and After the Pilgrims*. New York: Walker and Company, 1972.

Trigger, Bruce G., ed. *Handbook of North American Indians,* Vol. 15, *Northeast*. Washington, D. C.: Smithsonian Institution, 1978.

Underhill, Ruth. "Social organization of the Papago

Indians." *Columbia University Contributions of Anthropology, 30.* New York (1939).

Watkins, Frances E. *Hopi Toys.* Southwest Museum Leaflet, No. 19. Los Angeles, California (1946?).

————. *The Navajo.* Southwest Museum Leaflet, No. 16. Los Angeles, California (1943?).

Will, George F. and George E. Hyde. *Corn Among the Indians of the Upper Missouri.* Lincoln, Nebraska: University of Nebraska Press, 1964.

Index